Writings:
Prose And Poems
(Original And Translated)

by

Swami Vivekananda

ABOUT THE AUTHOR

Swami Vivekananda was born Narendranath Datta in India on January 12, 1863. He died on July 4, 1902, and was the most important student of the Indian saint Ramakrishna. He was an important part of bringing Vedanta and Yoga to the West. He is also charged with making people more aware of other religions and making Hinduism a major world religion. Vivekananda had a lot of success at the Parliament. In the years that followed, he gave hundreds of lectures across the United States, England, and Europe to spread the main ideas of Hinduism. He also started the Vedanta Society of New York and the Vedanta Society of San Francisco, which is now the Vedanta Society of Northern California. Both of these groups became the basis for Vedanta Societies in the West. Vivekananda was one of the most important philosophers and social reformers in India at the time. He was also one of the most successful and powerful Vedanta missionaries in the West.People now think of him as one of the most important people in modern India and Hinduism. Mahatma Gandhi said that after reading Vivekananda's works, he loved his country a thousand times more.

CONTENTS

Historical Evolution Of India 7

The Story Of The Boy Gopala 15

My Play Is Done 21

The Cup 24

A Benediction 25

The Hymn Of Creation 26

On The Sea's Bosom 27

Hinduism And Shri Ramakrishna 28

The Bengali Language 33

Matter For Serious Thought 36

Shiva's Demon 41

Historical Evolution Of India

OM TAT SAT

Om Namo Bhagavate Râmakrishnâya

नासतः सत् जायते — Existence cannot be produced by non-existence.

Non-existence can never be the cause of what exists. Something cannot come out of nothing. That the law of causation is omnipotent and knows no time or place when it did not exist is a doctrine as old as the Aryan race, sung by its ancient poet-seers, formulated by its philosophers, and made the corner-stone upon which the Hindu man even of today builds his whole scheme of life.

There was an inquisitiveness in the race to start with, which very soon developed into bold analysis, and though, in the first attempt, the work turned out might be like the attempts with shaky hands of the future master-sculptor, it very soon gave way to strict science, bold attempts, and startling results.

Its boldness made these men search every brick of their sacrificial altars; scan, cement, and pulverise every word of their scriptures; arrange, re-arrange, doubt, deny, or explain the ceremonies. It turned their gods inside out, and assigned only a secondary place to their omnipotent, omniscient, omnipresent Creator of the universe, their ancestral Father-in-heaven; or threw Him altogether overboard as useless, and started a world-religion without Him with even now the largest following of any religion. It evolved the science of geometry from the arrangements of bricks to build various altars, and startled the world with astronomical knowledge that arose from the attempts accurately to time their worship and oblations. It made their contribution to the science of mathematics the largest of any race, ancient or modern, and to their knowledge of chemistry, of metallic compounds in medicine, their scale of musical notes, their invention of the bow-instruments — (all) of great service in the building of modern European civilisation. It led them to invent the science of building up the child-mind through shining fables, of which every child in every civilised country learns in a nursery or a school and carries an impress through life.

Behind and before this analytical keenness, covering it as in a velvet sheath, was the other great mental peculiarity of the race — poetic insight. Its religion, its philosophy, its history, its ethics, its politics were all inlaid in a flower-bed of poetic imagery — the miracle of language which was called Sanskrit or "perfected", lending itself to expressing and manipulating them better than any other tongue. The aid of melodious numbers was invoked even to express the hard facts of mathematics.

This analytical power and the boldness of poetical visions which urged it onward are the two great internal causes in the make-up of the Hindu race. They together formed, as it were, the keynote to the national character. This combination is what is always making the race press onwards beyond the senses — the secret of those speculations which are like the steel blades the artisans used to manufacture — cutting through bars of iron, yet pliable enough to be easily bent into a circle.

They wrought poetry in silver and gold; the symphony of jewels, the maze of marble wonders, the music of colours, the fine fabrics which belong more to the fairyland of dreams than to the real — have back of them thousands of years of working of this national trait.

Arts and sciences, even the realities of domestic life, are covered with a mass of poetical conceptions, which are pressed forward till the sensuous touches the supersensuous and the real gets the rose-hue of the unreal.

The earliest glimpses we have of this race show it already in the possession of this characteristic, as an instrument of some use in its hands. Many forms of religion and society must have been left behind in the onward march, before we find the race as depicted in the scriptures, the Vedas.

An organised pantheon, elaborate ceremonials, divisions of society into hereditary classes necessitated by a variety of occupations, a great many necessaries and a good many luxuries of life are already there.

Most modern scholars are agreed that surroundings as to climate and conditions, purely Indian, were not yet working on the race.

Onwards through several centuries, we come to a multitude surrounded by the snows of Himalayas on the north and the heat of the south — vast plains, interminable forests, through which mighty rivers roll their tides. We catch a glimpse of different races — Dravidians, Tartars, and Aboriginals pouring in their quota of blood, of speech, of manners and religions. And at last a great nation emerges to our view — still keeping the type of the Aryan — stronger, broader, and more organised by the assimilation. We find the central assimilative core giving its type and character to the whole mass, clinging on with great pride to its name of "Aryan", and, though willing to give other races the benefits of its civilisation, it was by no means willing to admit them within the "Aryan" pale.

The Indian climate again gave a higher direction to the genius of the race. In a land where nature was propitious and yielded easy victories, the national mind started to grapple with and conquer the higher problems of life in the field of thought. Naturally the thinker, the priest, became the highest class in the Indian society, and not the man of the sword. The priests again, even at that dawn of history, put most of their energy in elaborating rituals; and when the nation began to find the load of ceremonies and lifeless rituals too heavy — came the first philosophical speculations, and the royal race was the first to break through the maze of killing rituals.

On the one hand, the majority of the priests impelled by economical considerations were bound to defend that form of religion which made their existence a necessity of society and assigned them the highest place in the scale of caste; on the other hand, the king-caste, whose strong right hand guarded and guided the nation and who now found itself as leading in the higher thoughts also, were loath to give up the first place to men who only knew how to conduct a ceremonial. There were then others, recruited from both the priests and king-castes, who ridiculed equally the ritualists and philosophers, declared spiritualism as fraud and priestcraft, and upheld the attainment of material comforts as the highest goal of life. The people, tired of ceremonials and wondering at the philosophers, joined in masses the materialists. This was the beginning of that caste question and that triangular fight in India between ceremonials, philosophy, and materialism which has come down unsolved to our own days.

The first solution of the difficulty attempted was by applying the eclecticism which from the earliest days had taught the people to see in differences the same truth in various garbs. The great leader of this school, Krishna — himself of royal race — and his sermon, the Gitâ, have after various vicissitudes, brought about by the upheavals of the Jains, the Buddhists, and other sects, fairly established themselves as the "Prophet" of India and the truest philosophy of life. Though the tension was toned down for the time, it did not satisfy the social wants which were among the causes — the claim of the king-race to stand first in the scale of caste and the popular intolerance of priestly privilege. Krishna had opened the gates of spiritual knowledge and attainment to all irrespective of sex or caste, but he left undisturbed the same problem on the social side. This again has come down to our own days, in spite of the gigantic struggle of the Buddhists, Vaishnavas, etc. to attain social equality for all.

Modern India admits spiritual equality of all souls — but strictly keeps the social difference.

Thus we find the struggle renewed all along the line in the seventh century before the Christian era and finally in the sixth, overwhelming the ancient order of things under Shâkya Muni, the Buddha. In their reaction against the privileged priesthood, Buddhists swept off almost every bit of the old ritual of the Vedas, subordinated the gods of the Vedas to the position of servants to their own human saints, and declared the "Creator and Supreme Ruler" as an invention of priestcraft and superstition.

But the aim of Buddhism was reform of the Vedic religion by standing against ceremonials requiring offerings of animals, against hereditary caste and exclusive priesthood, and against belief in permanent souls. It never attempted to destroy that religion, or overturn the social order. It introduced a vigorous method by organising a class of Sannyâsins into a strong monastic brotherhood, and the Brahmavâdinis into a body of nuns — by introducing images of saints in the place of altar-fires.

It is probable that the reformers had for centuries the majority of the Indian people with them. The older forces were never entirely pacified, but they underwent a good deal of modification during the centuries of Buddhistic supremacy.

In ancient India the centres of national life were always the intellectual and spiritual and not political. Of old, as now, political and social power has been always subordinated to spiritual and intellectual. The outburst of national life was round colleges of sages and spiritual teachers. We thus find the Samitis of the Panchâlas, of the Kâshyas (of Varanasi), the Maithilas standing out as great centres of spiritual culture and philosophy, even in tile Upanishads. Again these centres in turn became the focus of political ambition of the various divisions of the Aryans.

The great epic Mahâbhârata tells us of the war of the Kurus and Panchalas for supremacy over the nation, in which they destroyed each other. The spiritual supremacy veered round and centred in the East among the Magadhas and Maithilas, and after the Kuru-Panchala war a sort of supremacy was obtained by the kings of Magadha.

The Buddhist reformation and its chief field of activity were also in the same eastern region; and when the Maurya kings, forced possibly by the bar sinister on their escutcheon, patronised and led the new movement, the new priest power joined hands with the political power of the empire of Pataliputra. The popularity of Buddhism and its fresh vigour made the Maurya kings the greatest emperors that India ever had. The power of the

Maurya sovereigns made Buddhism that world-wide religion that we see even today.

The exclusiveness of the old form of Vedic religions debarred it from taking ready help from outside. At the same time it kept it pure and free from many debasing elements which Buddhism in its propagandist zeal was forced to assimilate.

This extreme adaptability in the long run made Indian Buddhism lose almost all its individuality, and extreme desire to be of the people made it unfit to cope with the intellectual forces of the mother religion in a few centuries. The Vedic party in the meanwhile got rid of a good deal of its most objectionable features, as animal sacrifice, and took lessons from the rival daughter in the judicious use of images, temple processions, and other impressive performances, and stood ready to take within her fold the whole empire of Indian Buddhism, already tottering to its fall.

And the crash came with the Scythian invasions and the total destruction of the empire of Pataliputra.

The invaders, already incensed at the invasion of their central Asiatic home by the preachers of Buddhism, found in the sun-worship of the Brahmins a great sympathy with their own solar religion — and when the Brahminist party were ready to adapt and spiritualise many of the customs of the new-comers, the invaders threw themselves heart and soul into the Brahminic cause.

Then there is a veil of darkness and shifting shadows; there are tumults of war, rumours of massacres; and the next scene rises upon a new phase of things.

The empire of Magadha was gone. Most of northern India was under the rule of petty chiefs always at war with one another. Buddhism was almost extinct except in some eastern and Himalayan provinces and in the extreme south and the nation after centuries of struggle against the power of a hereditary priesthood awoke to find itself in the clutches of a double priesthood of hereditary Brahmins and exclusive monks of the new regime, with all the powers of the Buddhistic organisation and without their sympathy for the people.

A renascent India, bought by the velour and blood of the heroic Rajputs, defined by the merciless intellect of a Brahmin from the same historical thought-centre of Mithila, led by a new philosophical impulse organised by Shankara and his bands of Sannyasins, and beautified by the arts and literature of the courts of Mâlavâ — arose on the ruins of the old.

The task before it was profound, problems vaster than any their ancestors had ever faced. A comparatively small and compact race of the same blood and speech and the same social and religious aspiration, trying to save its unity by unscalable walls around itself, grew huge by multiplication and addition during the Buddhistic supremacy; and (it) was divided by race, colour, speech, spiritual instinct, and social ambitions into hopelessly jarring factions. And this had to be unified and welded into one gigantic nation. This task Buddhism had also come to solve, and had taken it up when the proportions were not so vast.

So long it was a question of Aryanising the other types that were pressing for admission and thus, out of different elements, making a huge Aryan body. In spite of concessions and compromises, Buddhism was eminently successful and remained the national religion of India. But the time came when the allurements of sensual forms of worship, indiscriminately taken in along with various low races, were too dangerous for the central Aryan core, and a longer contact would certainly have destroyed the civilisation of the Aryans. Then came a natural reaction for self-preservation, and Buddhism and separate sect ceased to live in most parts of its land of birth.

The reaction-movement, led in close succession by Kumârila in the north, and Shankara and Râmânuja in the south, has become the last embodiment of that vast accumulation of sects and doctrines and rituals called Hinduism. For the last thousand years or more, its great task has been assimilation, with now and then an outburst of reformation. This reaction first wanted to revive the rituals of the Vedas — failing which, it made the Upanishads or the philosophic portions of the Vedas its basis. It brought Vyasa's system of Mimâmsâ philosophy and Krishna's sermon, the Gita, to the forefront; and all succeeding movements have followed the same. The movement of Shankara forced its way through its high intellectuality; but it could be of little service to the masses, because of its adherence to strict caste-laws, very small scope for ordinary emotion, and making Sanskrit the only vehicle of communication. Ramanuja on the other hand, with a most practical philosophy, a great appeal to the emotions, an entire denial of birthrights before spiritual attainments, and appeals through the popular tongue completely succeeded in bringing the masses back to the Vedic religion.

The northern reaction of ritualism was followed by the fitful glory of the Malava empire. With the destruction of that in a short time, northern India went to sleep as it were, for a long period, to be rudely awakened by the thundering onrush of Mohammedan cavalry across the passes of Afghanistan. In the south, however, the spiritual upheaval of Shankara and Ramanuja was followed by the usual Indian sequence of united races and powerful empires. It was the home of refuge of Indian religion and civilisation, when northern India from sea to sea lay bound at the feet of Central Asiatic conquerors. The Mohammedan tried for centuries to subjugate the south, but can scarcely be said to have got even a strong foothold; and when the strong and united empire of the Moguls was very near completing its conquest, the hills and plateaus of the south poured in their bands of fighting peasant horsemen, determined to die for the religion which Râmdâs preached and Tukâ sang; and in a short time the gigantic empire of the Moguls was only a name.

The movements in northern India during the Mohammedan period are characterised by their uniform attempt to hold the masses back from joining the religion of the conquerors — which brought in its train social and spiritual equality for all.

The friars of the orders founded by Râmânanda, Kabir, Dâdu, Chaitanya, or Nânak were all agreed in preaching the equality of man, however differing from each other in philosophy. Their energy was for the most part spent in checking the rapid conquest of Islam among the masses, and they had very little left to give birth to new thoughts and aspirations. Though evidently successful in their purpose of keeping the masses within the fold of the old religion, and tempering the fanaticism of the Mohammedans, they were mere apologists, struggling to obtain permission to live.

One great prophet, however, arose in the north, Govind Singh, the last Guru of the Sikhs, with creative genius; and the result of his spiritual work was followed by the well-known political organisation of the Sikhs. We have seen throughout the history of India, a spirtitual upheaval is almost always succeeded by a political unity extending over more or less area of the continent, which in its turn helps to strengthen the spiritual aspiration that brings it to being. But the spiritual aspiration that preceded the rise of the Mahratta or the Sikh empire was entirely reactionary. We seek in vain to find in the court of Poona or Lahore even a ray of reflection of that intellectual glory which surrounded the courts of the Muguls, much less the brilliance of Malava or Vidyânagara. It was intellectually the darkest period of Indian history; and both these meteoric empires, representing the upheaval of mass-fanaticism and hating culture with all their hearts, lost all their motive power as soon as they had succeeded in destroying the rule of the hated Mohammedans.

Then there came again a period of confusion. Friends and foes, the Mogul empire and its destroyers, and the till then peaceful foreign traders, French and English, all joined in a mêlée of fight. For more than half a century there was nothing but war and pillage and destruction. And when the smoke and dust cleared, England was stalking victorious over the rest. There has been half a century of peace and law and order under the sway of Britain. Time alone will prove if it is the order of progress or not.

There have been a few religious movements amongst the Indian people during the British rule, following the same line that was taken up by northern Indian sects during the sway of the empire of Delhi. They are the voices of the dead or the dying — the feeble tones of a terrorised people, pleading for permission to live. They are ever eager to adjust their spiritual or social surroundings according to the tastes of the conquerors — if they are only left the right to live, especially the sects under the English domination, in which social differences with the conquering race are more glaring than the spiritual. The Hindu sects of the century seem to have set one ideal of truth before them — the approval of their English masters. No wonder that these sects have mushroom lives to live. The vast body of the Indian people religiously hold aloof from them, and the only popular recognition they get is the jubilation of the people when they die.

But possibly, for some time yet, it cannot be otherwise.

The Story Of The Boy Gopala

"O mother! I am so afraid to go to school through the woods alone; other boys have servants or somebody to bring them to school or take them home — why cannot I have someone to bring me home?" — thus said Gopâla, a little Brahmin boy, to his mother one winter afternoon when he was getting ready for school. The school hours were in the morning and afternoon. It was dark when the school closed in the afternoon, and the path lay through the woods.

Gopala's mother was a widow. His father who had lived as a Brahmin should — never caring for the goods of the world, studying and teaching, worshipping and helping others to worship — died when Gopala was a baby. And the poor widow retired entirely from the concerns of the world — even from that little she ever had — her soul given entirely to God, and waiting patiently with prayers, fasting, and discipline, for the great deliverer death, to meet in another life, him who was the eternal companion of her joys and sorrows, her partner in the good and evil of the beginningless chain of lives. She lived in her little cottage. A small rice-field her husband received as sacred gift to learning brought her sufficient rice; and the piece of land that surrounded her cottage, with its clumps of bamboos, a few cocoanut palms, a few mangoes, and lichis, with the help of the kindly village folk, brought forth sufficient vegetables all the year round. For the rest, she worked hard every day for hours at the spinning-wheel.

She was up long before the rosy dawn touched the tufted heads of the palms, long before the birds had begun to warble in their nests, and sitting on her bed — a mat on the ground covered with a blanket — repeated the sacred names of the holy women of the past, saluted the ancient sages, recited the sacred names of Nârâyana the Refuge of mankind, of Shiva the merciful, of Târâ the Saviour Mother; and above all, (she) prayed to Him whom her heart most loved, Krishna, who had taken the form of Gopala, a cowherd, to teach and save mankind, and rejoiced that by one day she was nearer to him who had gone ahead, and with him nearer by a day to Him, the Cowherd.

Before the light of the day, she had her bath in the neighbouring stream, praying that her mind might be made as clean by the mercy of Krishna, as her body by the water. Then she put on her fresh-washed whiter cotton garment, collected some flowers, rubbed a piece of sandalwood on a circular stone with a little water to make a fragrant paste, gathered a few sweet-scented Tulasi leaves, and retired into a little room in the cottage, kept apart for worship. In this room she kept her Baby Cowherd; on a small wooden throne under a small silk canopy; on a small velvet cushion, almost covered with flowers, was placed a bronze image of Krishna as a baby. Her mother's heart could only be satisfied by conceiving God as her baby. Many and many a time her learned husband had talked to her of Him who is preached in the Vedas, the formless, the infinite, the impersonal. She listened with all attention, and the conclusion was always the same — what is written in the Vedas must be true; but, oh! it was so immense, so far off, and she, only a weak, ignorant woman; and then, it was also written: "In whatsoever form one seeks Me, I reach him in that form, for all mankind are but following the paths I laid down for them" — and that was enough. She wanted to know no more. And there she was — all of the devotion, of faith, of love her heart was capable of, was there in Krishna, the Baby Cowherd, and all that heart entwined round the visible Cowherd, this little bronze image. Then again she had heard: "Serve Me as you would a being of flesh and blood, with love and purity, and I accept that all." So she served as she would a master, a beloved teacher, above all, as she would serve the apple of her eye, her only child, her son.

So she bathed and dressed the image, burned incense before it, and for offering? — oh, she was so poor! — but with tears in her eyes she remembered her husband reading from the books: "I accept with gladness even leaves and flowers, fruits and water, whatever is offered with love", and she offered: "Thou for whom the world of flowers bloom, accept my few common flowers. Thou who feedest the universe, accept my poor offerings of fruits. I am weak, I am ignorant. I do not know how to approach Thee, how to worship Thee, my God, my Cowherd, my child; let my worship be pure, my love for Thee selfless; and if there is any virtue in worship, let it be Thine, grant me only love, love that never asks for anything — 'never seeks for anything but love'." Perchance the mendicant in his morning call was singing in the little yard:

Thy knowledge, man! I value not,
It is thy love I fear;
It is thy love that shakes My throne,
Brings God to human tear.

For love behold the Lord of all,
The formless, ever free,
Is made to take the human form
To play and live with thee.

What learning, they of Vrindâ's groves,
The herdsmen, ever got?
What science, girls that milked the kine?
They loved, and Me they bought.

Then, in the Divine, the mother-heart found her earthly son Gopala (lit. cowherd), named after the Divine Cowherd. And the soul which would almost mechanically move among its earthly surroundings — which, as it were, was constantly floating in a heavenly ether ready to drift away from contact of things material found its earthly moorings in her child. It was the only thing left to her to pile all her earthly joys and love on. Were not her movements, her thoughts, her pleasures, her very life for that little one that bound her to life?

For years she watched over the day-to-day unfolding of that baby life with all a mother's care; and now that he was old enough to go to school, how hard she worked for months to get the necessaries for the young scholar!

The necessaries however were few. In a land where men contentedly pass their lives poring over books in the the light of a mud lamp, with an ounce of oil in which is a thin cotton wick — a rush mat being the only furniture about them — the necessaries of a student are not many. Yet there were some, and even those cost many a day of hard work to the poor mother.

How for days she toiled over her wheel to buy Gopala a new cotton Dhoti and a piece of cotton Châdar, the under and upper coverings, the small mat in which Gopala was to put his bundle of palm leaves for writing and his reed pens, and which he was to carry rolled up under his arm to be used as his seat at school — and the inkstand. And what joy to her it was, when on a day of good omen Gopal attempted to write his first letters, only a mother's heart, a poor mother's, can know!

But today there is a dark shadow in her mind. Gopala is frightened to go alone through the wood. Never before had she felt her widowhood, her loneliness, her poverty so bitter. For a moment it was all dark, but she recalled to her mind what she had heard of the eternal promise: "Those that depend on Me giving up all other thoughts, to them I Myself carry whatever is necessary." And she was one of the souls who could believe.

So the mother wiped her tears and told her child that he need not fear. For in those woods lived another son of hers tending cattle, and also called Gopala; and if he was ever afraid passing through them, he had only to call on brother Gopala!

The child was that mother's son, and he believed.

That day, coming home from school through the wood, Gopala was frightened and called upon his brother Gopala, the cowherd: "Brother cowherd, are you here? Mother said you are, and I am to call on you: I am frightened being alone." And a voice came from behind the trees: "Don't be afraid, little brother, I am here; go home without fear."

Thus every day the boy called, and the voice answered. The mother heard of it with wonder and love; and she instructed her child to ask the brother of the wood to show himself the next time.

The next day the boy, when passing through the woods, called upon his brother. The voice came as usual, but the boy asked the brother in the woods to show himself to him. The voice replied, "I am busy today, brother, and cannot come." But the boy insisted, and out of the shade of the trees came the Cowherd of the woods, a boy dressed in the garb of cowherds, with a little crown on his head in which were peacock's feathers, and the cowherd's flute in his hands.

And they were so happy: they played together for hours in the woods, climbing trees, gathering fruits and flowers — the widow's Gopala and the Gopala of the woods, till it was almost late for school. Then the widow's Gopala went to school with a reluctant heart, and nearly forgot all his lesson, his mind eager to return to the woods and play with his brother.

Months passed this wise. The poor mother heard of it day by day and, in the joy of this Divine mercy, forgot her widowhood, her poverty, and blessed her miseries a thousand times.

Then there came some religious ceremonies which the teacher had to perform in honour of his ancestors. These village teachers, managing alone a number of boys and receiving no fixed fees from them, have to depend a great deal upon presents when the occasion requires them.

Each pupil brought in his share, in goods or money. And Gopala, the orphan, the widow's son! — the other boys smiled a smile of contempt on him when they talked of the presents they were bringing.

That night Gopala's heart was heavy, and he asked his mother for some present for the teacher, and the poor mother had nothing.

But she determined to do what she had been doing all her life, to depend on the Cowherd, and told her son to ask from his brother Gopala in the forests for some present for the teacher.

The next day, after Gopala had met the Cowherd boy in the woods as usual and after they had some games together, Gopala told his brother of the forest the grief that was in his mind and begged him to give him something to present his teacher with.

"Brother Gopala," said the cowherd, "I am only a cowherd you see, and have no money, but take this pot of cream as from a poor cowherd and present it to your teacher."

Gopala, quite glad that he now had something to give his teacher, more so because it was a present from his brother in the forest, hastened to the home of the teacher and stood with an eager heart behind a crowd of boys handing over their presents to the teacher. Many and varied were the presents they had brought, and no one thought of looking even at the present of the orphan.

The neglect was quite disheartening; tears stood in the eyes of Gopala, when by a sudden stroke of fortune the teacher happened to take notice of him. He took the small pot of cream from Gopala's hand, and poured the cream into a big vessel, when to his wonder the pot filled up again! Again he emptied the contents into a bigger vessel, again it was full; and thus it went on, the small pot filling up quicker than he could empty it.

Then amazement took hold of everyone; and the teacher took the poor orphan in his arms and inquired about the pot of cream.

Gopala told his teacher all about his brother Cowherd in the forest, how he answered his call, how he played with him, and how at last he gave him the pot of cream.

The teacher asked Gopala to take him to the woods and show him his brother of the woods, and Gopala was only too glad to take his teacher there.

The boy called upon his brother to appear, but there was no voice even that day. He called again and again. No answer. And then the boy entreated his brother in the forest to speak, else the teacher would think he was not speaking the truth. Then came the voice as from a great distance:

"Gopala, thy mother's and thy love and faith brought Me to thee; but tell thy teacher, he will have to wait a long while yet."

My Play Is Done

(Written in the Spring of 1895 in New York)

Ever rising, ever falling with the waves of time,
still rolling on I go
From fleeting scene to scene ephemeral,
with life's currents' ebb and flow.
Oh! I am sick of this unending force;
these shows they please no more.
This ever running, never reaching,
nor e'en a distant glimpse of shore!
From life to life I'm waiting at the gates,
alas, they open not.
Dim are my eyes with vain attempt
to catch one ray long sought.
On little life's high, narrow bridge
I stand and see below
The struggling, crying, laughing throng.
For what? No one can know.
In front yon gates stand frowning dark,
and say: "No farther way,
This is the limit; tempt not Fate,
bear it as best you may;
Go, mix with them and drink this cup
and be as mad as they.
Who dares to know but comes to grief;
stop then, and with them stay."
Alas for me. I cannot rest.
This floating bubble, earth —
Its hollow form, its hollow name,
its hollow death and birth —

For me is nothing. How I long
to get beyond the crust
Of name and form! Ah! ope the gates;
to me they open must.
Open the gates of light, O Mother, to me Thy tired son.
I long, oh, long to return home!
Mother, my play is done.
You sent me out in the dark to play,
and wore a frightful mask;
Then hope departed, terror came,
and play became a task.
Tossed to and fro, from wave to wave
in this seething, surging sea
Of passions strong and sorrows deep,
grief *is*, and joy *to be*,
Where life is living death, alas! and death —
who knows but 'tis
Another start, another round of this old wheel
of grief and bliss?
Where children dream bright, golden dreams,
too soon to find them dust,
And aye look back to hope long lost
and life a mass of rust!
Too late, the knowledge age cloth gain;
scarce from the wheel we're gone
When fresh, young lives put their strength
to the wheel, which thus goes on
From day to day and year to year.
'Tis but delusion's toy,
False hope its motor; desire, nave;
its spokes are grief and joy.
I go adrift and know not whither.
Save me from this fire!
Rescue me, merciful Mother, from floating with desire!
Turn not to me Thy awful face,
'tis more than I can bear.

Be merciful and kind to me,
to chide my faults forbear.
Take me, O Mother, to those shores
where strifes for ever cease;
Beyond all sorrows, beyond tears,
beyond e'en earthly bliss;
Whose glory neither sun, nor moon,
nor stars that twinkle bright,
Nor flash of lightning can express.
They but reflect its light.
Let never more delusive dreams
veil off Thy face from me.
My play is done, O Mother,
break my chains and make me free!

The Cup

This is your cup — the cup assigned
to you from the beginning.
Nay, My child, I know how much
of that dark drink is your own brew
Of fault and passion, ages long ago,
In the deep years of yesterday, I know.

This is your road — a painful road and drear.
I made the stones that never give you rest.
I set your friend in pleasant ways and clear,
And he shall come like you, unto My breast.
But you, My child, must travel here.

This is your task. It has no joy nor grace,
But it is not meant for any other hand,
And in My universe bath measured place,
Take it. I do not bid you understand.
I bid you close your eyes to see My face.

A Benediction

(Written to Sister Nivedita)

The mother's heart, the hero's will,
The sweetness of the southern breeze,
The sacred charm and strength that dwell
On Aryan altars, flaming, free;
All these be yours, and many more
No ancient soul could dream before —
Be thou to India's future son
The mistress, servant, friend in one.

The Hymn Of Creation

(A translation of the *Nâsadiya-Sukta*, Rig-Veda, X. 129.)

Existence was not then, nor non-existence,
The world was not, the sky beyond was neither.
What covered the mist? Of whom was that?
What was in the depths of darkness thick?

Death was not then, nor immortality,
The night was neither separate from day,
But motionless did *That* vibrate
Alone, with Its own glory one —
Beyond *That* nothing did exist.

At first in darkness hidden darkness lay,
Undistinguished as one mass of water,
Then *That* which lay in void thus covered
A glory did put forth by *Tapah*!

First desire rose, the primal seed of mind,
(The sages have seen all this in their hearts
Sifting existence from non-existence.)
Its rays above, below and sideways spread.

Creative then became the glory,
With self-sustaining principle below.
And Creative Energy above.

Who knew the way? Who there declared
Whence this arose? Projection whence?
For after this projection came the gods.
Who therefore knew indeed, came out this whence?

This projection whence arose,
Whether held or whether not,
He the ruler in the supreme sky, of this
He, O Sharman! knows, or knows not
He perchance!

On The Sea's Bosom

(Swami Vivekananda composed this poem in during his return from his second trip to the West. At the time of writing it, he was probably crossing the eastern Mediterranean.)

In blue sky floats a multitude of clouds —
White, black, of snaky shades and thicknesses;
An orange sun, about to say farewell,
Touches the massed cloud-shapes with streaks of red.

The wind blows as it lists, a hurricane
Now carving shapes, now breaking them apart:
Fancies, colours, forms, inert creations —
A myriad scenes, though real, yet fantastic.

There light clouds spread, heaping up spun cotton;
See next a huge snake, then a strong lion;
Again, behold a couple locked in love.
All vanish, at last, in the vapoury sky.

Below, the sea sings a varied music,
But not grand, O India, nor ennobling:
Thy waters, widely praised, murmur serene
In soothing cadence, without a harsh roar.

Hinduism And Shri Ramakrishna

By the word "Shastras" the Vedas without beginning or end are meant. In matters of religious duty the Vedas are the only capable authority.

The Puranas and other religious scriptures are all denoted by the word "Smriti". And their authority goes so far as they follow the Vedas and do not contradict them.

Truth is of two kinds: (1) that which is cognisable by the five ordinary senses of man, and by reasonings based thereon; (2) that which is cognisable by the subtle, supersensuous power of Yoga.

Knowledge acquired by the first means is called science; and knowledge acquired by the second is called the Vedas.

The whole body of supersensuous truths, having no beginning or end, and called by the name of the Vedas, is ever-existent. The Creator Himself is creating, preserving, and destroying the universe with the help of these truths.

The person in whom this supersensuous power is manifested is called a Rishi, and the supersensuous truths which he realises by this power are called the Vedas.

This Rishihood, this power of supersensuous perception of the Vedas, is real religion. And so long as this does not develop in the life of an initiate, so long is religion a mere empty word to him, and it is to be understood that he has not taken yet the first step in religion.

The authority of the Vedas extends to all ages, climes and persons; that is to say, their application is not confined to any particular place, time, and persons.

The Vedas are the only exponent of the universal religion.

Although the supersensuous vision of truths is to be met with in some measure in our Puranas and Itihasas and in the religious scriptures of other races, still the fourfold scripture known among the Aryan race as the Vedas being the first, the most complete, and the most undistorted collection of spiritual truths, deserve to occupy the highest place among all scriptures, command the respect of all nations of the earth, and furnish the rationale of all their respective scriptures.

With regard to the whole Vedic collection of truths discovered by the Aryan race, this also has to be understood that those portions alone which do not refer to purely secular matters and which do not merely record tradition or history, or merely provide incentives to duty, form the Vedas in the real sense.

The Vedas are divided into two portions, the Jnâna-kânda (knowledge-portion) and the Karma-kânda (ritual-portion). The ceremonies and the fruits of the Karma-kanda are confined within the limits of the world of Mâyâ, and therefore they have been undergoing and will undergo transformation according to the law of change which operates through time, space, and personality.

Social laws and customs likewise, being based on this Karma-kanda, have been changing and will continue to change hereafter. Minor social usages also will be recognised and accepted when they are compatible with the spirit of the true scriptures and the conduct and example of holy sages. But blind allegiance only to usages such as are repugnant to the spirit of the Shastras and the conduct of holy sages has been one of the main causes of the downfall of the Aryan race.

It is the Jnana-kanda or the Vedanta only that has for all time commanded recognition for leading men across Maya and bestowing salvation on them through the practice of Yoga, Bhakti, Jnana, or selfless work; and as its validity and authority remain unaffected by any limitations of time, place or persons, it is the only exponent of the universal and eternal religion for all mankind.

The Samhitas of Manu and other sages, following the lines laid down in the Karma-kanda, have mainly ordained rules of conduct conducive to social welfare, according to the exigencies of time, place, and persons. The Puranas etc. have taken up the truths imbedded in the Vedanta and have explained them in detail in the course of describing the exalted life and deeds of Avataras and others. They have each emphasised, besides, some out of the infinite aspects of the Divine Lord to teach men about them.

But when by the process of time, fallen from the true ideals and rules of conduct and devoid of the spirit of renunciation, addicted only to blind usages, and degraded in intellect, the descendants of the Aryans failed to appreciate even the spirit of these Puranas etc. which taught men of ordinary intelligence the abstruse truths of the Vedanta in concrete form and diffuse language and appeared antagonistic to one another on the surface, because of each inculcating with special emphasis only particular aspects of the spiritual ideal —

And when, as a consequence, they reduced India, the fair land of religion, to a scene of almost infernal confusion by breaking up piecemeal the one Eternal Religion of the Vedas (Sanâtana Dharma), the grand synthesis of all the aspects of the spiritual ideal, into conflicting sects and by seeking to sacrifice one another in the flames of sectarian hatred and intolerance —

Then it was that Shri Bhagavan Ramakrishna incarnated himself in India, to demonstrate what the true religion of the Aryan race is; to show where amidst all its many divisions and offshoots, scattered over the land in the course of its immemorial history, lies the true unity of the Hindu religion, which by its overwhelming number of sects discordant to superficial view, quarrelling constantly with each other and abounding in customs divergent in every way, has constituted itself a misleading enigma for our countrymen and the butt of contempt for foreigners; and above all, to hold up before men, for their lasting welfare, as a living embodiment of the Sanatana Dharma, his own wonderful life into which he infused the universal spirit and character of this Dharma, so long cast into oblivion by the process of time.

In order to show how the Vedic truths — eternally existent as the instrument with the Creator in His work of creation, preservation, and dissolution — reveal themselves spontaneously in the minds of the Rishis purified from all impressions of worldly attachment, and because such verification and confirmation of the scriptural truths will help the revival, reinstatement, and spread of religion — the Lord, though the very embodiment of the Vedas, in this His new incarnation has thoroughly discarded all external forms of learning.

That the Lord incarnates again and again in human form for the protection of the Vedas or the true religion, and of Brahminhood or the ministry of that religion — is a doctrine well established in the Puranas etc.

The waters of a river falling in a cataract acquire greater velocity, the rising wave after a hollow swells higher; so after every spell of decline, the Aryan society recovering from all the evils by the merciful dispensation of Providence has risen the more glorious and powerful — such is the testimony of history.

After rising from every fall, our revived society is expressing more and more its innate eternal perfection, and so also the omnipresent Lord in each successive incarnation is manifesting Himself more and more.

Again and again has our country fallen into a swoon, as it were, and again and again has India's Lord, by the manifestation of Himself, revivified her.

But greater than the present deep dismal night, now almost over, no pall of darkness had ever before enveloped this holy land of ours. And compared with the depth of this fall, all previous falls appear like little hoof-marks.

Therefore, before the effulgence of this new awakening' the glory of all past revivals in her history will pale like stars before the rising sun; and compared with this mighty manifestation of renewed strength, all the many past epochs of such restoration will be as child's play.

The various constituent ideals of the Religion Eternal, during its present state of decline, have been lying scattered here and there for want of competent men to realise them — some being preserved partially among small sects and some completely lost.

But strong in the strength of this new spiritual renaissance, men, after reorganising these scattered and disconnected spiritual ideals, will be able to comprehend and practice them in their own lives and also to recover from oblivion those that are lost. And as the sure pledge of this glorious future, the all-merciful Lord has manifested in the present age, as stated above, an incarnation which in point of completeness in revelation, its synthetic harmonising of all ideals, and its promoting of every sphere of spiritual culture, surpasses the manifestations of all past ages.

So at the very dawn of this momentous epoch, the reconciliation of all aspects and ideals of religious thought and worship is being proclaimed; this boundless, all embracing idea had been lying inherent, but so long concealed, in the Religion Eternal and its scriptures, and now rediscovered, it is being declared to humanity in a trumpet voice.

This epochal new dispensation is the harbinger of great good to the whole world, specially to India; and the inspirer of this dispensation, Shri Bhagavan Ramakrishna, is the reformed and remodelled manifestation of all the past great epoch-makers in religion. O man, have faith in this, and lay to heart.

The dead never return; the past night does not reappear; a spent-up tidal wave does not rise anew; neither does man inhabit the same body over again. So from the worship of the dead past, O man, we invite you to the worship of the living present; from the regretful brooding over bygones, we invite you to the activities of the present; from the waste of energy in retracing lost and demolished pathways, we call you back to broad new-laid highways lying very near. He that is wise, let him understand.

Of that power, which at the very first impulse has roused distant echoes from all the four quarters of the globe, conceive in your mind the manifestation in its fullness; and discarding all idle misgivings, weaknesses, and the jealousies characteristic of enslaved peoples, come and help in the turning of this mighty wheel of new dispensation!

With the conviction firmly rooted in your heart that you are the servants of the Lord, His children, helpers in the fulfilment of His purpose, enter the arena of work.

The Bengali Language

(Translated from Bengali)

(Written for the "Udbodhan")

In our country, owing to all learning being in Sanskrit from the ancient times, there has arisen an immeasurable gulf between the learned and the common folk. All the great personages, from Buddha down to Chaitanya and Ramakrishna, who came for the well-being of the world, taught the common people in the language of the people themselves. Of course, scholarship is an excellent thing; but cannot scholarship be displayed through any other medium than a language that is stiff and unintelligible, that is unnatural and merely artificial? Is there no room for art in the spoken language? What is the use of creating an unnatural language to the exclusion of the natural one? Do you not think out your scholastic researches in the language which you are accustomed to speak at home? Why then do you introduce such a queer and unwieldy thing when you proceed to put them in black and white? The language in which you think out philosophy and science in your mind, and argue with others in public — is not that the language for writing philosophy and science? If it is not, how then do you reason out those truths within yourselves and in company of others in that very language? The language in which we naturally express ourselves, in which we communicate our anger, grief, or love, etc.— there cannot be a fitter language than that. We must stick to that idea, that manner of expression, that diction and all. No artificial language can ever have that force, and that brevity and expressiveness, or admit of being given any turn you please, as that spoken language. Language must be made like pure steel — turn and twist it any way you like, it is again the same — it cleaves a rock in twain at one stroke, without its edge being turned. Our language is becoming artificial by imitating the slow and pompous movement — and only that — of Sanskrit. And language is the chief means and index of a nation's progress.

If you say, "It is all right, but there are various kinds of dialects in different parts of Bengal — which of them to accept?" — the answer is: We must accept that which is gaining strength and spreading through natural laws, that is to say, the language of Calcutta. East or west, from wheresoever people may come, once they breathe in the air of Calcutta, they are found to speak the language in vogue there; so nature herself points out which language to write in. The more railroads and facilities of communication there are, the more will the difference of east and west disappear, and from Chittagong to Baidyanath there will be that one language, viz that of Calcutta. It is not the question which district possesses a language most approaching Sanskrit — you must see which language is triumphing. When it is evident that the language of Calcutta will soon become the language of the whole of Bengal, then, if one has to make the written and spoken language the same, one would, if one is intelligent enough certainly make the language of Calcutta one's foundation. Here local jealousies also should be thrown overboard. Where the welfare of the whole province is concerned, you must overlook the claims to superiority of your own district or village.

Language is the vehicle of ideas. It is the ideas that are of prime importance, language comes after. Does it look well to place a monkey on a horse that has trappings of diamonds and pearls? Just look at Sanskrit. Look at the Sanskrit of the Brâhmanas, at Shabara Swâmi's commentary on the Mimâmsâ philosophy, the *Mahâbhâshya* of Patanjali, and, finally, at the great Commentary of Achârya Shankara: and look also at the Sanskrit of comparatively recent times. You will at once understand that so long as a man is alive, he talks a living language, but when he is dead, he speaks a dead language. The nearer death approaches, the more does the power of original thinking wane, the more is there the attempt to bury one or two rotten ideas under a heap of flowers and scents. Great God! What a parade they make! After ten pages of big adjectives, all on a sudden you have — "There lived the King!" Oh, what an array of spun-out adjectives, and giant compounds, and skilful puns! They are symptoms of death. When the country began to decay, then all these signs became manifest. It was not merely in language — all the arts began to manifest them. A building now neither expressed any idea nor followed any style; the columns were turned and turned till they had all their strength taken out of them. The ornaments pierced the nose and the neck and converted the wearer into a veritable ogress; but oh, the profusion of leaves and foliage carved fantastically in them! Again, in music, nobody, not even the sage Bharata, the originator of dramatic performances, could understand whether it was singing, or weeping, or wrangling, and what meaning or purpose it sought to convey! And what an abundance of intricacies in that music! What labyrinths of flourishes — enough to strain all one's nerves! Over and above that, that music had its birth in the nasal tone uttered through the teeth compressed, in imitation of the Mohammedan musical experts! Nowadays there is an indication of correcting these; now will people gradually understand that a language, or art, or music that expresses no meaning and is lifeless is of no good. Now they will understand that the more strength is infused into the national life, the more will language art, and music, etc. become spontaneously instinct with ideas and life. The volume of meaning that a couple of words of everyday use will convey, you may search in vain in two thousand set epithets. Then every image of the Deity will inspire devotion, every girl decked in ornaments will appear to be a goddess, and every house and room and furniture will be animated with the vibration of life.

Matter For Serious Thought

(*Translated from Bengali*)

A man presented himself to be blessed by a sight of the Deity. He had an access of joy and devotion at the sight; and perhaps to pay back the good he received, he burst out into a song. In one corner of the hall, reclining against a pillar, was Chobeji dozing. He was the priest in the temple, an athlete, a player on the guitar, was a good hand in swallowing two jugfuls of Bhâng (an intoxicating drink.), and had various other qualifications besides. All on a sudden, a dreadful noise assailing his tympanum, the fantastic universe conjured up under the influence of the inebriating liquor vanished for a moment from Chobeji's enormous chest of two and forty inches! And casting his crimson-tinged, languid eyes around in search of the cause of disturbance to his tranquil mind, Chobeji discovered that in front of the God was a man singing, overwhelmed with his own feelings, in a tune as touching as the scouring of cauldrons in a festive house, and, in so doing, he was subjecting the shades of the whole host of musical masters like Nârada, Bharata, Hanumân, Nâyaka, and the rest to ineffable anguish. The mortified Chobeji in a sharp reprimanding tone addressed the man who had been the direct obstacle to his enjoyment of that peculiar bliss of inebriation, "Hello, my friend, what are you shouting like that for, without caring for time or tune?" Quick came the response, "What need I care for time or tune? I am trying to win the Lord's heart." "Humph!" retorted Chobeji, "do you think the Lord is such a fool? You must be mad! You could not win my heart even — and has the Lord less brains than I?"

* * *

The Lord has declared unto Arjuna: "Take thou refuge in Me, thou hast nothing else to do. And I shall deliver thee." Bholâchand is mighty glad to hear this from some people; he now and then yells out in a trenchant note: "I have taken refuge in the Lord. I shall not have to do anything further." Bholachand is under the: impression that it is the height of devotion to bawl out those words repeatedly in the harshest tone possible. Moreover, he does not fail to make it known now and then in the aforesaid pitch that he is ever ready to lay down his life even, for the Lord's sake, and that if the Lord does not voluntarily surrender Himself to this tie of devotion, everything would be hollow and false. And a few foolish satellites of his also share the same opinion. But Bholachand is not prepared to give up a single piece of wickedness for the sake of the Lord. Well, is the Lord really such a fool? Why, this is not enough to hoodwink us even!

* * *

Bholâ Puri an out and out Vedantin — in everything he is careful to trumpet his Brahminhood. If all people are about to starve for food around Bhola Puri, it does not touch him even in the least; he expounds the unsubstantiality of pleasure and pain. If through disease, or affliction, or starvation people die by the thousand, what matters even that to him? He at once reflects on the immortality of the soul! If the strong overpower the weak and even kill them before his very eyes, Bhola Puri is lost in the profound depths of the meaning of the spiritual dictum, "The soul neither kills nor is killed." He is exceedingly averse to action of any kind. If hard pressed, he replies that he finished all actions in his previous births. But Bhola Puri's realisation of unity of the Self suffers a terrible check when he is hurt in one point. When there is some anomaly in the completeness of his Bhikshâ, or when the householder is unwilling to offer him worship according to his expectations, then, in the opinion of Puriji, there are no more despicable creatures on earth than householders, and he is at a loss to make out why the village that failed to offer adequate worship to him should, even for a moment add to the world's burden.

He, too, has evidently thought the Lord more foolish than ourselves.

* * *

"I say, Râm Charan, you have neither education nor the means to set up a trade, nor are you fit for physical labour. Besides, you cannot give up indulging in intoxications, nor do away with your wickednesses. Tell me, how do you manage to make your living?"

RAM CHARAN — "That is an easy job, sir; I preach unto all."

What has Ram Charan taken the Lord for?

* * *

The city of Lucknow is astir with the festivities of the Mohurrum. The gorgeous decorations and illumination in the principal mosque, the Imambara, know no bounds. Countless people have congregated. Hindus, Mohammedans, Christians, Jews — all sorts of people — men, women, and children of all races and creeds have crowded today to witness the Mohurrum. Lucknow is the capital of the Shias, and wailings in the name of the illustrious Hassan and Hossain rend the skies today. Who was there whose heart was not touched by the lamentation and beating of breasts that took place on this mournful occasion? The tale of the Kârbâlâ, now a thousand years old, has been renovated today.

Among this crowd of spectators were two Rajput gentlemen, who had come from a far-off village to see the festival. The Thakur Sahibs were — as is generally the case with village zemindârs (landlords) — innocent of learning. That Mohammedan culture, the shower of euphuistic phraseology with its nice and correct pronunciation, the varieties of fashionable dress — the loose-fitting cloaks and tight trousers and turbans, of a hundred different colours, to suit the taste of the townsfolk — all these had not yet found their way to such a remote village to convert the Thakur Sahibs. The Thakurs were, therefore, simple and straightforward, always fond of hunting, stalwart and hardy, and of exceedingly tough hearts.

The Thakurs had crossed the gate and were about to enter the mosque, when the guard interrupted them. Upon inquiring into the reasons, he answered, "Look here, this giant figure that you see standing by the doorway, you must give it five kicks first, and then you can go in." "Whose is the statue, pray?" "It is the statue of the nefarious Yejid who killed the illustrious Hassan and Hossain a thousand years ago. Therefore is this crying and this mourning." The guard thought that after this elaborate explanation the statue of Yejid was sure to merit ten kicks instead of five. But mysterious are the workings of Karma, and everything was sadly misunderstood. The Thakurs reverentially put their scarfs round their neck and prostrated and rolled themselves at the feet of the statue of Yeiid, praying with faltering accents: "What is the use of going in any more? What other gods need be seen? Bravo Yejid! Thou alone art the true God. Thou hast thrashed the rascals so well that they are weeping till now!"

* * *

There is the towering temple of the Eternal Hindu Religion, and how many ways of approaching it! And what can you not find there? From the Absolute Brahman of the Vedantin down to Brahma, Vishnu, Shiva, Shakti, Uncle Sun, (The Sun is popularly given this familiar appellation.) the rat-riding Ganesha, and the minor deities such as Shashthi and Mâkâl, and so forth — which is lacking there? And in the Vedas, in the Vedanta, and the Philosophies, in the Puranas and the Tantras, there are lots of materials, a single sentence of which is enough to break one's chain of transmigration for ever. And oh, the crowd! Millions and millions of people are rushing towards the temple. I, too, had a curiosity to see and join in the rush. But what was this that met my eyes when I reached the spot! Nobody was going inside the temple! By the side of the door, there was a standing figure, with fifty heads, a hundred arms, two hundred bellies, and five hundred legs, and everyone was rolling at the feet of that. I asked one for the reason and got the reply: "Those deities that you see in the interior, it is worship enough for them to make a short prostration, or throw in a few flowers from a distance. But the real worship must be offered to him who is at the gate; and those Vedas, the Vedanta, and the Philosophies, the Puranas and other scriptures that you see — there is no harm if you hear them read now and then; but you must obey the mandate of this one." Then I asked again, "Well, what is the name of this God of gods?" "He is named Popular Custom" — came the reply. I was reminded of the Thakur Sahibs, and exclaimed, "Bravo, Popular Custom! Thou hast thrashed them so well", etc.

* * *

Gurguré Krishnavyâl Bhattâchârya is a vastly learned man, who has the knowledge of the whole world at his finger-ends. His frame is a skeleton; his friends say it is through the rigours of his austerities, but his enemies ascribe it to want of food. The wicked, again, are of opinion that such a physique is but natural to one who has a dozen issues every year. However that may be, there is nothing on earth that Krishnavyal does not know; specially, he is omniscient about the flow of electric magnetic currents all over the human body, from the hair-tuft to its furthest nook and corner. And being possessed of this esoteric knowledge, he is incomparably the best authority for giving a scientific explanation all things — from a certain earth used in the worship of the goddess Durga down to the reasonable age of puberty of a girl being ten, and sundry inexplicable and mysterious rites pertaining to allied matters. And as for adducing precedents, well, he has made the thing so clear that even boys could understand it. There is forsooth no other land for religion than India, and within India itself none but the Brahmins have the qualification for understanding religion and among Brahmins, too, all others excepting the Krishnavyal family are as nothing and, of these latter again, Gurguré has the pre-eminent claim! Therefore whatever Gurguré Krishnavyal says is self-evident truth.

Learning is being cultivated to a considerable extent, and people are becoming a bit conscious and active, so that they want to understand anal taste everything; so Krishnavyal is assuring everybody: "Discard all fear! Whatever doubts are arising in your minds, I am giving scientific explanations for them. You remain just as you were. Sleep to your heart's content and never mind anything else. Only, don't forget my honorarium." The people exclaimed: "Oh, what a relief! What a great danger did really confront us! We should have had to sit up, and walk, and move — what a pest!" So they said, "Long live Krishnavyal", and turned on one side on the bed once more. The habit of a thousand years was not to go so soon. The body itself would resent it. The inveterate obtuseness of the mind of a thousand years was not to pass away at a moment's notice. And is it not for this that the Krishnavyal class are held in repute? "Bravo, Habit! Thou hast thrashed them so well", etc.

Shiva's Demon

(This incomplete story was found among Swamiji's
papers after he had passed away. It is printed as
the last article in the Bengali book *Bhâbbâr Kathâ*.)

Baron K— lived in a district of Germany. Born in all aristocratic family,
he inherited high rank, honour and wealth even in early youth; besides, he
was highly cultured and endowed with many accomplishments. A good
many charming, affluent, and young women of rank craved for his love. And
which father or mother does not wish for a son-in-law of such parts, culture,
handsomeness, social position, lineage, and youthful age? An aristocratic
beauty had attracted Baron K— also, but the marriage was still far off. In
spite of all rank and wealth, Baron K— had none to call his own, except a
sister who was exquisitely beautiful and educated. The Baron had taken a
vow that he would marry only after his sister had chosen her fiancé and the
marriage celebrated with due éclat and rich dowries from him. She had been
the apple of her parents' eyes. Baron K— did not want to enjoy a married
life, before her wedding. Besides, the custom in this Western country is that
the son does not live in his father's or in any relative's family after marriage;
the couple live separately. It may be possible for the husband to live with
his wife in his father-in-law's house but a wife will never live in her father-
in-law's. So K— postponed his marriage till his sister's.

* * *

For some months K— had no news of his sister. Foregoing the life
of ease, comfort, and happiness in a palace served by a big retinue, and
snatching herself from the affection of her only brother, she had absconded.
All search had been in vain. That brought K— untold sorrow. He had no
more any relish for the pleasures of life; he was ever unhappy and dejected.
His relatives now gave up all hope of the sister's return, and tried to make

the Baron cheerful. They were very anxious about him, and his fiancee was ever full of apprehension.

* * *

It was the time of the Paris Exhibition. The *élite* of all countries assembled there. The art-treasures, and artistic products were brought to Paris from all quarters. Baron K—'s relatives advised him to go to Paris where his despondent heart would regain its normal health and buoyancy, once it was in contact with that active, invigorating current of joy. The Baron bowed down to their wishes and started for Paris with his friends.